Companion Bible Study for Run

Finding Friends & Handling Bullies

What Others are Saying . . .

Glenn Haggerty has mined an exceptional work of fiction to dig into the crucial issues of friendship, rejection, bullying and relationship with God. Readers young and not so young will be gripped by its fresh perspective and biblical insight.

Dave Johnson
Lead Pastor, *River of Life Church*

I loved this study! It addresses such an important need, not only bullying but also the issue of using force.

Dr. Gene Wilson
Church Planting Director, *ReachGlobal*
Co-author of *Global Church Planting. Biblical Principles and Best Practices for Multiplication*. Baker Academic 2011

As a parent of three teenagers, I want to help them grow in their faith and apply it to real-life situations. The study my friend Glenn Haggerty wrote does both. Your teen will love it and so will you. As a parent and pastor, I encourage you to work through this study with your teen. It will be a shared experience that will help you to connect and learn with them.

John Braland
Lead Pastor, Freshwater Community Church

Other Books by Glenn Haggerty

Escape, Intense Book 1

Run, Intense Book 2

Chase, Intense Book 3

Companion Bible Study for Run

Finding Friends & Handling Bullies

by

Glenn Haggerty

freshwater

Freshwater Publications
St. Bonifacius, Minnesota

ISBN 978-0-9993994-5-3 (print)
978-0-9993994-6-0 (eBook)

freshwater

Freshwater Publications
St. Bonifacius, Minnesota

1 3 5 7 9 10 8 6 4 2

Dedication

To every lonely child and teen longing for solid friendships.

Table of Contents

Table of Contents

Introduction

This study provides biblical principles to equip students to improve friendships and better deal with bullying situations.

This Companion Study Accompanies

Run, Intense Book 2

ISBN 978-0-9993994-7-7 (print)

or 978-0-9993994-8-4 (e-book)

Available at Amazon and Barnes & Noble

The Study

Proverbs tells us, "*A friend is always loyal, and a brother is born to help in time of need*" (17:17). In the novel, *Run*, thirteen-year-old Tyler Higgins goes from unhealthy friendships to no friendships to finally fitting in. This companion study explores where Tyler went wrong, where he went right, and how teens and preteens can develop real relationships. It also delves deeply into the issue of bullying which continues to trouble kids and teens. Because of the complexities of bullying, three sessions are devoted to this subject, including, *Ten Biblical Tips for Dealing with Bullies*, and why no one deserves to be disrespected.

Reading the action adventure novel, *Run,* Intense Book 2, concurrently with this study is ideal, but not necessary. Students can complete this study individually. However, a group setting or one-on-one with parents or another adult mentor would enrich the experience.

Run, Intense Book 2, the Novel

Tyler Higgins made some blunders and burned some bridges. Can he build a new life after he moves from Florida to a small northern town in the middle of nowhere? Or will he repeat his past mistakes?

Like the twisted trails crisscrossing the forest behind the Higgins' new home, Tyler's destiny is woven together with the mysterious plumbers. Trouble lurks behind every bend, as these criminals threaten his life and his family. Can Tyler find the wisdom, faith and courage to overcome? Will he achieve his ultimate goal – to fit in?

Run shows one young teen's battle to survive the pitfalls of adolescent life—and the dangers in the dark forest. Parents and people of all ages will also enjoy the heart pounding action and relational angst of *Run*.

Leader's Guide

Instructions for group leaders are printed in the appendix of this study.

Getting Started

This Bible study is designed for ten to fourteen-year-old boys and girls. Each session explores a key issue with a key scripture followed by a series of search the scripture questions. Each session also includes response and prayer sections, and as a side note, cool backstory to the novel *Run*.

Materials – Students

- Each student will need a copy of this seven-session bible study, *Companion Bible Study for Run, Finding Friends & Handling Bullies*. Scripture verses for each question are included in the back of the study.

- Each student should also have a copy of the novel, *Run*, Intense Book 2, and ideally read it before answering the questions. However, as an alternative, students can read the *Chapter Summaries* included in the appendix of this study.

Using this Study

Students can use this study as a daily devotional, reading the materials and answering a question or two per day, or complete each session in one sitting. Each of the seven sessions covers approximately five chapters of the novel, *Run*, which students should read before answering the questions.

- Scripture verses for the questions are printed at the end of the study guide.

- Answer each as honestly as you can based on the scripture and information from the story.

- Be sure to read the *How Will You Respond* section at the end of each lesson and record your planned action steps to the study.

- Record prayer requests.

- The *Cool Backstory & Fun Factoids* sections are on-your-own readings for fun.
- *Chapter Summaries* and answers to the questions are included in the *Leader's Guide* in the appendix.
- Due to the reflowable nature of ebooks, the page numbers of the ebook of this study are not the same as those of the print version. Please encourage those using the ebook to utilize the Table of Contents to navigate between book sections.

For I can do everything through Christ, who gives me strength.

(Philippians 4:13 NLT).

SESSION 1: Finding Friends

***RUN* Chapters 1-5**

ICE BREAKERS

1. Have you ever been lost, really lost in the woods or somewhere else? Can you remember that feeling of panic that Tyler and Dylan felt? How did you find your way home?
2. Have you ever had to make new friends with kids you didn't know? How did you feel about it at the time? Can you remember anything specific that helped you feel welcome?

Key Issue: Finding Friends

Don't be selfish.

New home, new school, and new neighbors, Tyler focused on the older and cooler Matt and would do almost anything to fit in—including take risks, use his brother and ignore other people he thought might get in his way. For Tyler, it was all about Tyler.

SEARCH THE SCRIPTURES

1. Tyler demonstrated two friendship blockers in this section. First, he thought he was so cool he could only hang out with the other "cool" kids. Consider Proverbs 29:23. How

do people feel about other people who act like they're too good for them?

2. Tyler thought he was too good for Luke. Have you ever thought you were too good for someone? What does God think about that according to Galatians 3:26-28?

3. Respect other's space. Tyler's second friendship blocker was trying too hard. Have you ever known someone who wanted to be with you all the time—I mean ALL the time? How did that make you feel?

4. Contentment brings confidence. Read Philippians 4:11-13, could you be content without friends for a time? How?

5. Tyler obsessed over befriending the older and cooler Matt. Has desire for something or someone ever so filled your mind that it led you to make dumb choices? Read Philippians 4:6-9 and list some ways you can treat "obsession."

6. *"Don't be too proud to enjoy the company of ordinary people"* (Romans 12:16). Have you ever gotten to know someone you had thought was unlikable or uninteresting and then discovered that he or she was different but fascinating? Is there such a person in your life whose friendship you could learn to enjoy this week?

Key Verse: Philippians 2:3

Don't be selfish; don't try to impress others. Be humble, thinking of others as better than yourselves.

How Will You Respond?

Jay Kessler used to say, "If you want a friend, be a friend." Rather than trying to *get* a friend like Tyler did in the novel, *be* a friend to those around you, in your church, youth group, school and other team and social activities. Take an interest in other people. Ask questions about their lives, be a good listener and you will never run out of things to talk about! On the other hand, don't appear too desperate—that usually drives people away. Remember, you can't please everybody so don't try pushing yourself on people who aren't interested.

Could you pray for someone, besides yourself, who needs a friend today? Could *you* be the friend that person needs?

Cool Backstory & Fun Factoids

Introducing: Tyler Higgins

Naturally shy, Tyler sometimes stumbles over words and feels awkward—until he connects with friends. He owns in soccer and video games, but he still yearns to join the in-crowd at school and fears being labeled as a nerd. During seventh grade at Palm Aire Christian Academy the in-crowd was ruled by a skeptical jerk named Dustin.

Dustin pretended friendship to trick Tyler into doing something stupid. Then he blackmailed Tyler into betraying his friend, Nathan. By the time Tyler figured things out, he had lost his friendship with Nathan. And Dustin, after ruining Tyler's friendships, ditched him too.

Now with a midsummer move between seventh and eighth grade, Tyler gets to start over in Lehigh, a small town in the middle of nowhere.

The Ruined House

Every year, people abandon thousands of homes in the US, including remote rural properties. The county eventually forecloses and auctions them off to collect back taxes. Many don't sell, leaving the county with the deed.

So the county owns The Ruined House, and it lays forgotten until Packman, Frank and Runyon's prison mate from Attica, secretly took possession on his first parole. He expanded the cellar, added a tunnel and additional underground chambers—all in preparation for a nasty business. But police nailed Packman for breaking parole and returned him to Attica Prison. There Runyon, who hated the little pervert, broke his neck and staged it as an accident—but not before Frank wheedled directions to the property from Packman.

If Packman had been honest, he might have obtained title to the property through "the law of adverse possession." Essentially anyone who openly possesses property without the owner's permission can gain legal title after as few as five years in some states.

Notes

Notes

SESSION 2: Forgiving Friends

***RUN* Chapters 6-10**

ICE BREAKERS

1. When you're stressed-out where do you go to relax? How do you take your mind off of your problems?

2. Why didn't Tyler tell someone about the Plumber's threat with the knife in the dark? What would you have done?

Key Issue: Forgiving Friends

Unforgiveness poisons friendships—and distances God when we need Him most.

Someone has said, "To err is human, to forgive is divine." Perhaps believers are never more Christ-like than when they forgive those who have wronged them. Forgiving others is not optional but can be incredibly difficult. Often forgiveness doesn't happen in an instant, rather it requires time and focused effort. And forgiveness doesn't mean you immediately grant trust to the person who has offended you, for trust once broken must be earned again. But believers have a secret weapon in this matter that the world knows nothing about!

SEARCH THE SCRIPTURES

1. Angry feelings are often unavoidable; it's what we *do* with our anger that makes the difference. How could advice from James 1:19 have helped Tyler in his anger?

2. Read our key verse again (Colossians 3:13). Are believers always required to forgive others? Why or Why not?

3. Read Ephesians 4:26-27, 31. When anger controls a person, what does that look like? How does anger give the devil a foothold in our lives?

4. Anger if not released in forgiveness leads to bitterness. Read Hebrews 12:15b. What effect does bitterness have on people? Are bitter people fun to be around?

5. Arguably, Matt and Ryan's dirty trick was funny. But kicking Tyler, Dylan, and Luke off this public fishing spot and stealing their fish was mean. Read Romans 12:14. Have you ever tried to bless and pray for those who persecute you? What were the short-term results? Can you think of any long-term benefits?

6. Proverbs 11:12 says, *"It is foolish to belittle one's neighbor; a sensible person keeps quiet."* After the booger incident, why was Tyler so hot on dissing Luke to Dylan?

7. According to Matthew 6:14-15, what happens to a believer's relationship with God when he or she refuses to forgive another person? What happened to Tyler when he refused to forgive Luke?

Key Verse: Colossians 3:13

Make allowance for each other's faults, and forgive anyone who offends you. Remember, the Lord forgave you, so you must forgive others.

How Will You Respond?

Like Tyler, we are hardwired for relationships. Everyone needs to talk with like persons, feel accepted and share real concern. Refusing to forgive can destroy friendships that could otherwise be great fun.

Like Dylan, have you ever held a grudge against someone, even though they were sorry? If you haven't already, what would it look like for you to make that right?

"Bless those who curse you. Pray for those who hurt you." (Luke 6:28). Prayer is the believer's secret weapon. Will you pray for those who have offended you?

Cool Backstory & Fun Factoids

Introducing: Dylan Higgins

Dylan, Tyler's chatterbox eleven-year-old brother, never lacked friends. Unlike his brother, Dylan is friendly, honest and kind (except to Tyler sometimes). A willful fire often lights his green eyes and colors the small scar over his left eye—earned while trying to keep up with big brother on the scooter. Dylan plays soccer, likes music and building with Legos, and dislikes being bossed around by big bro—he also holds grudges.

Introducing: Luke Franklin

Twelve-year-old Luke is a friendly bookworm with a fun imagination and no brothers or sisters. He avoids scoffers, doesn't care about the in-crowd, and is content with school, church youth group and a few friends. Luke also likes to play Legos and music but doesn't like the forest. His father teaches English at the public middle school in Henderson, and his mom, Lisa, works part-time at the Pharmaceutical Company.

Lehigh

A town of about 600 people, lays in a grid shape on the east and west side of Main Street. Highway 33 enters Lehigh from the south, becomes Main Street through the downtown, and after crossing the shallow, swift-flowing river becomes Riverside Drive. Tyler Higgins lives across the river about half a mile outside of town. After walking south over the bridge, he'd see Hank's Pizzeria, a convenience store, City Hall and Sam's Hardware fronting Main Street. The eastward curve of Main Street hides McDonald's and several other stores further south. But from the bridge, Tyler could also see Mesner's Bait Shop just before Riverview Park. The three-story offices of Lehigh Medical and Pharmaceutical Supply, the town's largest employer, lay several blocks west of Main Street.

Notes

Notes

SESSION 3: Facing Bullies Part 1

***RUN* Chapters 11-15**

Key Issue: Bullies

How do you handle bullies?

Tyler had to deal with bullies early on. Bullying is inflicting repeated and unwanted insults, threats, or physical force upon another. Despite the efforts of parents and school officials, the age-old problem of bullying persists. Whether shoves, curses and threats in the hallway or lies, rumors and spoofing through text and social networks, kids still say and do incredibly mean things to other kids—maybe even more so when they can pretend to be someone else in cyberspace.

How do you respond?

SEARCH THE SCRIPTURES

Ten Biblical Tips for Dealing with Bullies

1. **The Audacious Truth—You Don't Deserve Bullying**

   You are God's masterpiece, unique, one-of-a-kind, and created in His image! You are beloved by God, and He has a *special purpose* for your life that only you can fulfill.

   a. Read the second part of Genesis 9:6. Why is it wrong to take or harm a human life? Why would it be wrong to allow others to abuse you physically or verbally?

b. Bullies want power over others and what they have. They will use threats, violence and lies to get it. But what goes around comes around. What does Galatians 6:7 say bullies should ultimately expect? Have you ever seen bullies themselves bullied or punished in other ways for their bullying?

c. According to 2 Peter 3:9, why is God's justice sometimes delayed?

d. Proverbs 14:15 says, *"Only simpletons believe everything they're told!"* And 2 Corinthians 10:5b teaches us to bring every negative thought into captivity. Discuss how we can practically control the negative thoughts that bullies or anyone else have placed inside our heads.

2. Prayer, the Believer's Secret Weapon

As you pray for others, pray for yourself. Don't accept lies that bullies heap upon you. Rather renounce them to yourself and to the bullies.

a. Read Luke 6:28. Tyler didn't bless Blake and his posse, but he didn't curse them either and eventually he even prayed for them. Have you ever prayed for someone who persecuted you? How did that change your attitude? Your situation?

3. **Identify and Avoid—be alert to bullying activities and avoid them.**
   a. Read Proverbs 22:3. What did Tyler do to avoid Blake and Nick? Can you think of other ways of avoiding bullies?

Bullying comes in different stages, and your response should differ accordingly.

Early Stages of Bullying

4. **Ignore and Don't Retaliate**
   a. The Bible says there is, "*A time to be quiet and a time to speak*" (Ecclesiastes 3:7b). Often the strongest and wisest action is to ignore an insult, taunt or challenge. How well did Tyler do ignoring Blake's insults?

b. "*Don't retaliate with insults when people insult you*" (1 Peter 3:9b). It's super hard not to lash back when insulted. But according to Proverbs 15:1, what happens when people retaliate?

c. How did Tyler react to Nick's taunts the next day in class? What was Nick's reaction? How might it have played out if Tyler had ignored Nick? We discuss how he could have responded to Nick but without retaliation in the next tip.

5. Practice a Gentle Answer

Anticipate the bullies taunt and practice a nonconfrontational answer. Role-playing may feel weird at first, but practicing answers aloud with another person can powerfully prepare you for the next unavoidable confrontation, so ask a trusted adult for help. "*A gentle answer deflects anger*" (Proverbs 15:1a). If you have truly offended someone, apologize! On the other hand, DO NOT accept lies about yourself. Therefore, a neutral answer when taunted, such as "That didn't sound nice," or "That sounded unkind (or seems bigoted, racist, etc.) don't you think?" or "are you bullying me?" may be the best way to deflect a bully's hostility. Instead of calling Nick "pepperoni face," Tyler could have responded with "most of us have pimples at one time or another, but don't you think it's mean to point that out?" Instead of calling Nick a coward, Tyler could have said, "Were you helping to bully that little kid or were you just watching?"

a. What are some other ways you can respond to insults, taunts and threats without accepting a lie about yourself, or stirring up anger in the bully?

6. Leave with Confidence

Leave with confidence. A confident retreat is another strategy for dealing with bullies. Jesus told the disciples that if people wouldn't welcome or listen to them to, "*shake the dust off your feet when you leave that home or town* (Matthew 10:14). Telling bullies in a confident tone, "Excuse me, I need to leave," (or "I'm out," "see ya," "gotta go," "whatever") communicates strength, an unwillingness to accept abuse and is nonconfrontational.

a. When confronted by a bully in or out of school, where are some places you can go to get away? We'll talk about what to do if you're trapped somewhere, like on a bus, in tips number eight and following in the next session.

b. Tyler walked away from Blake in their second confrontation in the hallway but he also looked over his shoulder. Why is it important to stay alert even as you walk away from a bully?

7. **Do Something Nice**

   Most kids will feel guilty if they return meanness for help. So do something nice for the bully—but not in a moment of confrontation. Rather do it unexpectedly so the bully will see your motivation as being nice and not fear. A real compliment can also be a game changer when the opportunity arises. And yet there is a line between toadying to get the bully off of your back and sincere compliments.

   a. *"Instead, pay them back with a blessing"* (1 Peter 3:9c). Have you ever said something nice to someone after he or she said something mean about you? How did that change the situation?

Key Verse: Ephesians 2:10

For we are God's masterpiece. He has created us anew in Christ Jesus, so we can do the good things he planned for us long ago.

How Will You Respond?

All of these tips need to be applied with wisdom; different situations may call for different responses. Where can you get that wisdom according to James 1:5?

James also denounces poisonous words—cursing people because God made everyone in His image. He says of the tongue,

***It is restless and evil, full of deadly poison. Sometimes it praises our Lord and Father, and sometimes it curses those who have been made in the image of God. And so blessing and cursing come pouring out of the same mouth. Surely, my brothers and sisters, this is not right!* (James 3:8b-10).**

It's not right. The word "curse" here means to declare someone evil or loathsome. You were made in the image of God—his masterpiece. It's not right to allow someone to declare you evil or loathsome.

Are bullies getting you down so deep you can't see the surface? If you are suffering at the hands of bullies—please get help now! Don't let those negative words and abuse take root in your mind and change who you are.

Cool Backstory & Fun Factoids

Introducing: Matt Colter

Matt is fourteen and a half, stoutly built and four inches taller than Tyler, but with his playful blue eyes, he looked like an angel. At first, Matt seemed friendly, however, behind the pleasant smile hid a practical joker with a little meanness sprinkled in. Matt was a tough football player and a bad enemy—most kids didn't mess with him. He won't back down from a fight but has a deep sense of fair play.

The Academy

A K-9 charter school, The Academy has about 180 students that crowd the halls of 436 Huron Street. Located on a wooded knoll a block west of Main Street, the school is about a three-quarter of a mile walk for the Higgins kids. Shrubs enclose the front courtyard and left side, while a small playground straddles the right side of this two-acre campus. A small auditorium attaches to the rear of the horseshoe shaped structure. But with limited land, The Academy uses the city's ball fields south of the property for most outdoor sports.

Notes

SESSION 4: Facing Bullies Part 2

***RUN* Chapters 11-15**

ICE BREAKER

1. Has anybody ever missed, or been tempted to miss, school, church, or other activities for fear of bullying?

Key Issue: Bullies

How do you handle bullies?

Again, bullying is inflicting repeated and unwanted insults, threats, coercion, or physical force upon another. Tyler wasn't experiencing cyberbullying—yet, he didn't have a cell phone, and his Internet connections were still limited. But he was the target of social bullying, exclusion, gossip and insults. The last session we discussed how we are each made in God's image—one of His amazing masterpieces. As God's children, we are also loved—even cherished and created for a mission that only we can fulfill.

SEARCH THE SCRIPTURES

Ten Biblical Tips for Dealing with Bullies

We previously covered why you don't deserve bullying, and the Biblical tips of prayer, identifying and avoiding, ignoring and non-retaliation, a gentle answer, leaving with confidence and doing something nice. Here are the next three tips. As with the first seven, these too must be applied with wisdom (James 1:5) and not necessarily in order.

Bullying sometimes escalates.

Advanced Stages of Bullying

Sometimes avoiding, ignoring, gentle answers, and doing something nice do not deter bullies. Like wolves scenting blood, when kids sense weakness, they'll sometimes pile on with a pack mentality. At this stage seek help from trusted adults. And lies, rumors, and cyberbullying almost always need adult intervention.

8. **Get Adult Help**

   Bullies can't always be avoided. When bullying escalates, always appeal to your parents or other responsible adults for help. When confronted by a mob that was trying to trick Paul into an ambush, he appealed to the Roman authorities for help (Acts 25:11).

   a. Tyler never did tell the school authorities about Blake's bullying. If he had, how might it have changed the situation?

   b. However, Tyler finally told Dad, and it made a huge difference, but you'll have to read the next section to find out how! Are you enduring a bullying situation that you should talk over with your parents or other adults? Will you?

9. **Stand Up to Bullies**

Sometimes you should stand up to bullies. When Paul was confronted with a flogging, he simply asked, *"Is it legal for you to whip a Roman citizen who hasn't even been tried?"* (Acts 22:25). That was a game changer and extricated Paul from a terrible situation. Similarly, ask tormentors **questions that indirectly confront**. For example; "What would the principal/pastor say if someone was videoing you right now?" or "Did you know that the Internet and phone companies keep a permanent record of all texts and photos? And they always give it up to police when asked."

a. When and how did Tyler stand up to Blake and Nick? How did that work for him?

b. Speaking up—loudly at times may be called for. Have you ever heard someone say in a loud voice, "stop bullying me!" or something like that? When would that work? When would it not work?

c. Should you be concerned when bullies target someone else? Read Proverbs 31:8-9. Who would you speak with first, an adult, the bullies, or the crowd?

In chapter seventeen of *Run,* Tyler is forced to stand up to the bully. The next session (five) will cover how Tyler did that, and the issue of self-defense.

10. Flee

If you can't get adequate adult help—run! Jesus said on one occasion to flee persecution (Matthew 10:23). Exercise judgment but fleeing a dangerous situation—and then reporting the threat to adults is usually the wisest strategy.

a. Name and discuss some situations that call for flat out running from danger, versus taking a stand or a controlled retreat.

b. What happened when Tyler made a controlled retreat to the student pickup area in his first confrontation with Blake? If Blake held a weapon how would that have changed the situation?

Has anyone experienced cyberbullying? Discuss how you could stand up to, or flee online insults, rumors, threats, or coercion.

Key Verse: Ephesians 2:10

For we are God's masterpiece. He has created us anew in Christ Jesus, so we can do the good things he planned for us long ago.

How Will You Respond?

Cyberbullying. Any text, photo or message you send or post can be captured, spread all over Cyberspace and used against you! SO BE CAREFUL WHAT YOU SAY AND SEND ONLINE! Conversely, when people spread rumors, insult, threaten or try to coerce you online, TELL your parents or another trusted adult. This can get dangerous and nasty real fast. You may not even know who you are really communicating with.

Self-defense is another action point for dealing with bullies. In the next lesson, *Bullying Part 3*, we'll address this controversial issue from a Biblical perspective.

Resources

The following resources are for the reader's convenience and do not signify endorsement. Many other resources are available online, and from libraries, school officials, and medical care providers.

Kidpower www.kidpower.org/bullying/

Focus on the Family
www.focusonthefamily.com/parenting/schooling/bullying/bullying

Stop Bullying Now Foundation
stopbullyingnowfoundation.org

So Not Okay: An Honest Look at Bullying from the Bystander (Mean Girl Makeover Book 1) **by Nancy Rue**
www.nancyrue.com

Notes

SESSION 5: Facing Bullies Part 3

***RUN* Chapters 16-20**

Key Issue: Fight or flight

Should Christians defend themselves? If so, how? And when?

Retaliation vs. Self-Defense

Retaliation means striking back and hurting others because they have hurt you.

Self-defense, on the other hand, means preventing others from hurting you or others.

Retaliation was the accepted norm in Jesus' time. Zealots and Pharisees alike taught that when harmed, you had the right to strike back, even with violence. But Jesus emphatically condemned revenge and taught against resisting personal aggression. For Jesus allowed himself to be insulted, spit upon and finally crucified. As imitators of Christ, He also calls believers to endure persecution. For the Apostle commends believers who suffer for doing good (1 Peter 2:19). But is nonresistance of aggression an absolute principle?

SEARCH THE SCRIPTURES

1. Read John 18:20-23. Did Jesus turn the other cheek when struck?

Although Jesus didn't physically resist, he challenged his persecutors with questions, and the Apostle Paul rebuked his tormentors for slapping him (Acts 23:3). Forgiveness and nonresistance against personal persecution are Christian norms, as are love and prayer for enemies. However, in the context of the Matthew passage and the entire scripture, there are other factors to consider.

2. Are believers called upon to defend the weak? Read Psalm 82:3-4.

3. According to John 2:14-16, did Jesus use force to resist evil aggressively? What kind of force?

4. Were the Apostles prepared to use force for self-defense? Did Jesus approve? Read Luke 22:36-38.

5. Christians are called to be peacemakers. However, is it always possible to obtain peace with others? Read Romans 12:18. Why or why not?

6. According to Romans 12:19, can individual Christians ever avenge themselves?

Use of Force and Self-Defense

Jesus reserved his highest praise for a Roman Centurion—a professional soldier (Matthew 8:10). Rome paid this man to use his sword to keep the peace, and yet there is no evidence that Jesus commanded him to forsake soldiering and its attending violence. So too the Apostles applauded and accepted Cornelius—another Roman Centurion (Acts 10).

7. In Luke 3:14 repentant soldiers asked John the Baptist for instructions following their baptism. What did John say? Did he instruct them to quit the army or forsake soldierly duties?

8. What danger can you expect if you use force, especially lethal force against another? Read Matthew 26:52.

Key Verse: Matthew 5:39

But I say, do not resist an evil person! If someone slaps you on the right cheek, offer the other cheek also.

How Will You Respond?

How does this apply to dealing with playground bullies? Read Romans 12:18 again. Is self-defense implied if you cannot maintain peace? King David said, "Praise the Lord, who is my rock. He trains my hands for war and gives my fingers skill for battle" (Psalm 144:1). When conflict seemed inevitable with Blake, what did Tyler do?

In summary, on the playground, peacemakers should apply kindness, prayer and gentle answers to keep the peace. When that fails, appeal to adults and authorities to intervene. However, when bullies prey upon the weak, and adults cannot or will not intervene, then deliver the oppressed if you can do so. If bullies persecute you personally and the above mentioned does not suffice, then turning the other cheek may be the most powerful demonstration for Jesus and end for the bullying. However, if turning the other cheek doesn't end the bullying, then the Holy Spirit may direct believers to use force for self-defense—but never retaliate, and always forgive.

Pray about it. If you feel God calling you to learn self-defense, talk to your parents.

Cool Backstory & Fun Factoids

Introducing: Mike Higgins

Tall and still lean at age thirty-eight, Mr. Higgins strokes his chin when concentrating and never cusses. He was born in upstate New York and relocated to Florida as a teen. After graduating from college, he married his sweetheart, Laura, and spent the next 15 years as a management consultant. He relocated to Lehigh for its central location in his new territory. Mike is strong, a good talker, and has faith. But he tends toward work-a-holism and is often absent. Still, he loves his wife and children.

Lunchroom

Double doors entering the L-shaped lunch room are centered on the long wall. Rows of tables parallel the doors, with a broad aisle leading down the center of the room. Another set of tables bank against the far back wall perpendicular to the other tables. To the left side, a door leads to the kitchen. An open counter on the near back wall separates the lunchroom from the kitchen. A small variety of lunches are served at the counters. A vending machine with juice and milk is in the left corner at the bottom of the L with another single exit door to the right. Tyler was trapped in the back of the lunchroom, cut off from both doors by Blake and his posse, and out of sight of the kitchen which was empty at the time anyway.

Notes

SESSION 6: Sacrifice for Friends

RUN Chapters 21-24

Key Issue: Self-sacrifice and Friendship

Self-sacrifice means giving up something we have or want for the benefit of another. It is a demonstration of love and leads to deep bonds of friendship.

God hardwired people for relationships. We not only want to communicate and hang out with others on a meaningful level, but we also need friendships for mental and spiritual health. From the very beginning, God said it wasn't good for man to be alone (Genesis 2:18). And the entire message of the Bible is God's desire and plan to restore relationship with humankind. And that restoration includes rebuilding relationships between people. God's greatest commandment is to Love God—and the second is to love one another.

SEARCH THE SCRIPTURES

1. On the slope, Tyler proved his love by giving up his chance to escape to save his friends. Did Tyler pray for help? How many ways did God respond to Tyler's need?

2. Laying down your life for a friend doesn't necessarily mean literally dying. Describe some situations where you

can give up your plans for another's good—and the good of your friendship?

3. Read 1 Corinthians 13:4-7, and list the attributes of love that you SHOULD DO. Which attributes are most difficult for you to do daily? Which ones are the easiest?

4. From the same passage, list the things you SHOULD AVOID. Which things are most difficult for you to avoid daily? Which ones are the easiest?

5. And of those listed in one and two above, rank the ones you would like others to apply to you first.

6. *"A gossip goes around telling secrets, but those who are trustworthy can keep a confidence"* and *". . . Gossip separates the best of friends"* (Proverbs 11:13, 16:28b).

Read Philippians 2:3-5. How can you develop an attitude that will help you to avoid gossip and disrespecting others?

7. People make mistakes and offend one another. Session two highlighted the need for forgiveness, both of self and of others who've offended us. Read Ephesians 4:32 again. Why are Christians able to forgive others?

8. According to 1 Thessalonians 5:11, what is another practical and positive thing you can do to develop friendships? What would encouraging another person look like to you today?

Key Verse: John 15:13

There is no greater love than to lay down one's life for one's friends.

How Will You Respond?

God desires that we develop meaningful friendships. Any urges that pull us toward isolation are not of God. One of Satan's strategies for defeating people is to tear down their relationships. We must, therefore, fight through unhealthy urges toward isolation, or behaviors that hurt relationships and seek other believers in Christian friendship. "No man is an island."

List one action step from today's study that you will put into practice this week.

Cool Backstory & Fun Factoids

Introducing: Frank Messina

Always smallish growing up, Frank carefully conceals a chip on his shoulder. When bullied as a child, he sucked-up for survival while secretly plotting payback. His revenge ranged from stealing fellow students' property to vandalizing lockers to hacking into computers and planting mischief. As an older teen he graduated to sabotaging automobiles—and his favorite, arson. Frank was arrested three times before being convicted of burning down a row house and sent to Attica for life.

Kolokol-1

The mysterious knockout drug Kolokol-1 may actually exist. A reputed derivative of the anesthetic, Fentanyl, Kolokol was developed by the Russian military to render targets unconscious. Rumor has it that the Russians used the aerosol in an anti-terrorist mission. However, such powerful knockout drugs can so suppress breathing that targets and hostages alike die. And yet, knockout gas is still popularized by movies, TV and works of fiction such as *Run*. On the other hand, could the U.S. and Russian military really have such a secret weapon?

Cell Phone Jammers

A cell phone jammer blocks cell phone signals with a switch of a button. A portable, battery operated phone jammer the size of a scientific calculator can block 3G and 4G signals within a range of 20 yards. For bigger jobs, a mountable plug-in unit can block cell phones within 50 to 100 yards. This type of jammer can be used continuously to block cell phone usage within a specific area, such as a school.

Notes

Notes

SESSION 7: Talk to God

RUN Chapters 25-27

Good news, God wants your company! He speaks to his children primarily through his word, the Bible. Then he wants us to reply, sharing our inner thoughts and feelings in prayer. Prayer can be profoundly simple, such as Peter's *"Save me, Lord!"* (Matthew 14:30) or detailed like the nearly 1,200-word Levitical prayer recorded in Nehemiah chapter nine.

There is a certain mystery to prayer. God is in control, yet He expects His children to pray. Talking to God is crucial to the believer's life, affecting spiritual growth, and has a radical effect in both the earthly and spiritual realms.

Key Issue: Prayer

Prayer is simply talking to God—and He's always there, always listening. But how do we pray?

At the beginning of *Run*, Tyler wasn't talking to God much. By the end, he talked to God—a lot—and saw some pretty amazing things happen. How can believers pray effectively, and experience the presence and power of God?

SEARCH THE SCRIPTURES

In Matthew chapter six, the Lord Jesus taught us how to pray by providing a model known as "The Lord's Prayer," a misnomer since it is actually the disciples' prayer.

1. Read Matthew 6:9-13 According to verse nine, how should believers address God? What does that tell you about how God views you? *Note ascribing holiness to God's name is a form of praise.*

2. In verse ten, believers yield their wills to God. What do you think will happen when God's Kingdom comes? Are you willing to align yourself with God's will? What might that look like in your next week?

3. Who can pray to God according to John 1:12 and Matthew 7:9-11? Are you one of God's children? If you are unsure, ask a trusted adult how you can be sure.

4. Prayer usually includes four parts:

    1. Praising God
    2. Confessing sins
    3. Thanking God
    4. Making requests for yourself and others.

Match the four parts of prayer to the appropriate following verses.

a. 1 John 1:9

b. Matthew 7:7-8

c. Ephesians 5:20

d. Psalm 103:1-2

5. According to Psalm 66:18, why is it so important to confess our sins to God regularly?

6. Jesus usually found a place where he could be alone to pray. Do you have a place where you can be alone and safe to talk to God without distractions? Could you share where?

7. List specific occasions when believers should pray according to the following.
   a. James 5:13

   b. Philippians 4:6

   c. Matthew 26:41

8. Which prayers will God always answer with a yes according to 1 John 5:14-15 and which will he usually answer with a no? (see James 4:2-3)

9. Tyler prayed for a miracle for Will's parents. Which principles in this study did he apply?

Key Verses: Mark 11:24-25

I tell you, you can pray for anything, and if you believe that you've received it, it will be yours. But when you are praying, first forgive anyone you are holding a grudge against, so that your Father in heaven will forgive your sins, too.

How Will You Respond?

Have you ever not prayed for a miracle because you were afraid of disappointment if God answered no? Christians talk about the power of prayer, but how much time do believers actually spend praying? In the early church, believers devoted themselves to prayer, along with fellowship, communion and the study of God's word (Acts 2:42). When the disciples gathered to pray, the results were sometimes so powerful that the room shook, angels showed up, and miracles occurred.

How about you? How often throughout the day do you "talk to God" as you would talk to your parents or a friend? Can you kick that up a notch today?

How much time do you spend in alert prayer per day?

Cool Backstory & Fun Factoids

Introducing: Will Fuller

Will, normally a fun-loving chatterbox, has become fearful and insecure. He lives with his father, Dr. Joseph Fuller, a handsome medical doctor with bespectacled dark eyes. A congenial atheist, Dr. Fuller scoffs at Christians and his attitude has affected Will. Two years previously Dr. Fuller fell into infidelity, and Will's parents divorced. Joseph repented and sought reconciliation; however, his wife, Carla, would have none of it. She relocated about fifteen miles away with Will, who still attends Henderson Middle School. Two weeks previously, an auto accident left Carla in a coma at Henderson Memorial Hospital. She's not expected to live, and Dr. Fuller took Will full time.

Silencers

As a hardened killer, Runyon had the equipment, including a silencer for his 9mm handgun. Silencers aren't standard for the Beretta 9mm. First, the barrel sight has to be adjusted so a gunsmith can machine grooves into the tip of the barrel. A suppression muzzle such as the Wraith YHM QD manufactured by various weapons specialty companies can then be securely screwed onto the barrel. But a suppression muzzle alone only reduces the roar of a 9mm round. To get that movie theater, "thunk, thunk," suppression ammunition is also required.

Night Vision Goggles

The military and law enforcement routinely utilize ambient light accessed through night vision goggles such as the Select Alpha image intensifiers, AN/PVS-7-SA. Its single tube, bi-ocular configuration has sophisticated controls, including a demist shield and headgear to hold the bulky binocular in place. Interestingly, such equipment is available to hunters in handheld versions or rifle mounted night vision.

Conclusion

If you want a friend, be a friend. And if you want to keep a friend, then forgive a friend. Remember, you are God's masterpiece, and he has a special plan and assignment for your life—one only you can fulfill. So, don't let anyone disrespect or bully you. God will hear your prayers and grant you the wisdom, strength and help you need to deal with bullies.

Love others, regardless of where they are from or who they are. Treat them like you'd want them to treat you. And talk to God, he loves you more than you can ever know and promises never to leave or forsake you.

Biblical principles work! Apply them and experience the abundant life God wants for his children.

Want to be sure you are a child of God? CRU has an easy-to-understand explanation of how to become God's child—to know him personally and intimately. Check it out at: **www.cru.org/how-to-know-god/would-you-like-to-know-god-personally.html**

Notes

Did you enjoy this study?

If so, would you take a quick minute to leave a review? It needn't be long. Just a sentence or two saying what you liked about the study!

Your recommendation would be a huge encouragement to me and help others to find this book.

SCRIPTURE VERSES

SESSION 1

Philippians 2:3 Don't be selfish; don't try to impress others. Be humble, thinking of others as better than yourselves.

Proverbs 29:23 Pride ends in humiliation, while humility brings honor.

Galatians 3:26-28 For you are all children of God through faith in Christ Jesus. And all who have been united with Christ in baptism have put on Christ, like putting on new clothes. There is no longer Jew or Gentile, slave or free, male and female. For you are all one in Christ Jesus.

Philippians 4:11-13 Not that I was ever in need, for I have learned how to be content with whatever I have. I know how to live on almost nothing or with everything. I have learned the secret of living in every situation, whether it is with a full stomach or empty, with plenty or little. For I can do everything through Christ, who gives me strength.

Philippians 4:6-9 Don't worry about anything; instead, pray about everything. Tell God what you need, and thank him for all he has done. Then you will experience God's peace, which exceeds anything we can understand. His peace will guard your hearts and minds as you live in Christ Jesus. And now, dear brothers and sisters, one final thing. Fix your thoughts on what is true, and honorable, and right, and pure, and lovely, and admirable. Think about things that are excellent and worthy of praise. Keep putting into practice all you learned and received from me—everything you heard from me and saw me doing. Then the God of peace will be with you.

Romans 12:16 Live in harmony with each other. Don't be too proud to enjoy the company of ordinary people. And don't think you know it all!

SESSION 2

Colossians 3:13 Make allowance for each other's faults, and forgive anyone who offends you. Remember, the Lord forgave you, so you must forgive others.

James 1:19 Understand this, my dear brothers and sisters: You must all be quick to listen, slow to speak, and slow to get angry.

Ephesians 4:26-27, 31 And "don't sin by letting anger control you." Don't let the sun go down while you are still angry, for anger gives a foothold to the devil.

Get rid of all bitterness, rage, anger, harsh words, and slander, as well as all types of evil behavior.

Hebrews 12:15b Watch out that no poisonous root of bitterness grows up to trouble you, corrupting many.

Romans 12:14 Bless those who persecute you. Don't curse them; pray that God will bless them.

Proverbs 11:12 It is foolish to belittle one's neighbor; a sensible person keeps quiet.

Matthew 6:14-15 If you forgive those who sin against you, your heavenly Father will forgive you. But if you refuse to forgive others, your Father will not forgive your sins.

SESSION 3

Genesis 9:6 If anyone takes a human life, that person's life will also be taken by human hands. For God made human beings in his own image.

Galatians 6:7 Don't be misled—you cannot mock the justice of God. You will always harvest what you plant.

2 Peter 3:9 The Lord isn't really being slow about his promise, as some people think. No, he is being patient for your sake. He does not want anyone to be destroyed, but wants everyone to repent.

1 Corinthians 10:5b We capture their rebellious thoughts and teach them to obey Christ

Luke 6:28 Bless those who curse you. Pray for those who hurt you.

Proverbs 22:23 A prudent person foresees danger and takes precautions. The simpleton goes blindly on and suffers the consequence.

Proverbs 15:1 A gentle answer deflects anger, but harsh words make tempers flare.

James 1:5 If you need wisdom, ask our generous God, and he will give it to you. He will not rebuke you for asking.

SESSION 4

Acts 25:11 "If I have done something worthy of death, I don't refuse to die. But if I am innocent, no one has a right to turn me over to these men to kill me. I appeal to Caesar!"

Proverbs 31:8-9 Speak up for those who cannot speak for themselves; ensure justice for those being crushed. Yes, speak up for the poor and helpless, and see that they get justice.

Matthew 10:23 When you are persecuted in one town, flee to the next.

SESSION 5

1 Peter 2:19 For God is pleased with you when you do what you know is right and patiently endure unfair treatment.

Matthew 5:39 But I say, do not resist an evil person! If someone slaps you on the right cheek, offer the other cheek also.

John 18:20-23 Jesus replied, "Everyone knows what I teach. I have preached regularly in the synagogues and the Temple, where the people gather. I have not spoken in secret. Why are you asking me this question? Ask those who heard me. They know what I said." Then one of the Temple guards standing nearby slapped Jesus across the face. "Is that the way to answer the high priest?" he demanded. Jesus replied, "If I said anything wrong, you must prove it. But if I'm speaking the truth, why are you beating me?"

Acts 23:3 But Paul said to him, "God will slap you, you corrupt hypocrite! What kind of judge are you to break the law yourself by ordering me struck like that?"

Psalm 82:3-4 Give justice to the poor and the orphan; uphold the rights of the oppressed and the destitute. Rescue the poor and helpless; deliver them from the grasp of evil people.

John 2:14-16 In the Temple area he saw merchants selling cattle, sheep, and doves for sacrifices; he also saw dealers at tables exchanging foreign money. Jesus made a whip from some ropes and chased them all out of the Temple. He drove out the sheep and cattle, scattered the money changers' coins over the floor, and turned over their tables. Then, going over to the people who sold doves, he told them, "Get these things out of here. Stop turning my Father's house into a marketplace!"

Luke 22:36-38 "But now," he said, "take your money and a traveler's bag. And if you don't have a sword, sell your cloak and buy one! For the time has come for this prophecy about me to be fulfilled: 'He was counted among the rebels.' Yes, everything written about me by the prophets will come true."

"Look, Lord," they replied, "we have two swords among us."

"That's enough," he said.

Romans 12:18 Do all that you can to live in peace with everyone.

Romans 12:19 Dear friends, never take revenge. Leave that to the righteous anger of God. For the Scriptures say, "I will take revenge; I will pay them back," says the Lord.

Matthew 8:10 When Jesus heard this, he was amazed. Turning to those who were following him, he said, "I tell you the truth, I haven't seen faith like this in all Israel!"

Luke 3:14 "What should we do?" asked some soldiers. John replied, "Don't extort money or make false accusations. And be content with your pay."

Matthew 26:52 Put away your sword," Jesus told him. "Those who use the sword will die by the sword."

SESSION 6

Genesis 2:18 Then the Lord God said, "It is not good for the man to be alone. I will make a helper who is just right for him."

John 15:13 There is no greater love than to lay down one's life for one's friends.

1 Corinthians 13:4-7 Love is patient and kind. Love is not jealous or boastful or proud or rude. It does not demand its own way. It is not irritable, and it keeps no record of being wronged. It does not rejoice about injustice but rejoices whenever the truth wins out. Love never gives up, never loses faith, is always hopeful, and endures through every circumstance.

Proverbs 16:28 A troublemaker plants seeds of strife; gossip separates the best of friends

Philippians 2:3-5 Don't be selfish; don't try to impress others. Be humble, thinking of others as better than yourselves. Don't look out only for your own interests, but take an interest in others, too. You must have the same attitude that Christ Jesus had.

Ephesians 4:32 Instead, be kind to each other, tenderhearted, forgiving one another, just as God through Christ has forgiven you.

1 Thessalonians 5:11 So encourage each other and build each other up, just as you are already doing.

SESSION 7

Matthew 14:30 But when he saw the strong wind and the waves, he was terrified and began to sink. "Save me, Lord!" he shouted.

Matthew 6:9-14 Pray like this: Our Father in heaven, may your name be kept holy. May your Kingdom come soon. May your will be done on earth, as it is in heaven. Give us today the food we need, and forgive us our sins, as we have forgiven those who sin against us. And don't let us yield to temptation, but rescue us from the evil one. If you forgive those who sin against you, your heavenly Father will forgive you.

John 1:12 But to all who believed him and accepted him, he gave the right to become children of God.

Matthew 7:9-11 You parents—if your children ask for a loaf of bread, do you give them a stone instead? Or if they ask for a fish, do you give them a snake? Of course not! So if you sinful people know how to give good gifts to your children, how much more will your heavenly Father give good gifts to those who ask him!

1 John 1:9 But if we confess our sins to him, he is faithful and just to forgive us our sins and to cleanse us from all wickedness.

Matthew 7:7-8 Keep on asking, and you will receive what you ask for. Keep on seeking, and you will find. Keep on knocking, and the door will be opened to you. For everyone who asks, receives. Everyone who seeks, finds. And to everyone who knocks, the door will be opened.

Ephesians 5:20 And give thanks for everything to God the Father in the name of our Lord Jesus Christ.

Psalm 103:1-2 Let all that I am praise the Lord; with my whole heart, I will praise his holy name. Let all that I am praise the Lord; may I never forget the good things he does for me.

Psalm 68:18 If I had not confessed the sin in my heart, the Lord would not have listened.

James 5:13 Are any of you suffering hardships? You should pray. Are any of you happy? You should sing praises.

Philippians 4:6 Don't worry about anything; instead, pray about everything. Tell God what you need, and thank him for all he has done.

Matthew 26:41 Keep watch and pray, so that you will not give in to temptation. For the spirit is willing, but the body is weak!

1 John 5:14-15 And we are confident that he hears us whenever we ask for anything that pleases him. And since we know he hears us when we make our requests, we also know that he will give us what we ask for.

James 4:2-3 You want what you don't have, so you scheme and kill to get it. You are jealous of what others have, but you can't get it, so you fight and wage war to take it away from them. Yet you don't have what you want because you don't ask God for it. And even when you ask, you don't get it because your motives are all wrong—you want only what will give you pleasure.

Acts 2:42 All the believers devoted themselves to the apostles' teaching, and to fellowship, and to sharing in meals (including the Lord's Supper), and to prayer.

Acts 4:31 After this prayer, the meeting place shook, and they were all filled with the Holy Spirit. Then they preached the word of God with boldness.

LEADER'S GUIDE

Included in this Leader's Guide

- Leaders Instructions
- *Chapter Summaries* for each session
- Answers to the questions for the leader's use

GETTING STARTED

This Bible study is designed for seven 60-minute sessions, including 15 minutes for the leader to read chapter excerpts from the novel, *Run,* Intense Book 2.

Target audience: Ten- to fourteen-year-old boys and girls.

Each session explores a key issue and scripture followed by five to ten questions. The lessons also include response and prayer sections, and cool backstory to the novel *Run*.

Materials – Leader

- The leader will need a copy of, *Companion Bible Study for Run, Finding Friends and Handling Bullies,* which includes the *Scripture Verses*, the *Leader's Guide*, *Chapter Summaries* and *Answer Guide* (for the leader's use).

- The leader should have a copy of the novel, *Run,* Intense Book 2.

Materials – Students

- Each student needs a copy of, *Companion Bible Study for Run, Finding Friends and Handling Bullies.* Scripture verses for the questions are printed in the back of the study.

- Optional. Each student should also have a copy of the novel, *Run,* Intense Book 2, and ideally read it before answering the questions. Students who haven't read the novel may read the *Chapter Summaries* located in the following section of this *Leader's Guide.*

LEADER RESPONSIBILITIES

The leader doesn't necessarily teach, but rather facilitates the discussion, and need not have extensive Bible knowledge.

- The leader will organize the study, including signup and ordering materials.

- Become familiar with the Bible study materials, answer the questions, read the *Chapter Summaries*, and optionally read the novel, *Run*.

- Lead the study. Optionally begin the group session with a 15-minute reading from the novel, *Run* (see the reading selections listed below for each session).

- Read or ask students to read the *Key Issue*, *Key Scripture*, questions and tips for each session.

- Encourage students to answer the questions (even if they haven't done so in advance) and share them with the group.

- Record prayer requests.

- Read the, *How Will You Respond*, section at the end of each lesson and challenge the students to take action steps.
- The *Cool Backstory & Fun Factoids* sections are on-your-own readings for the students, except for Sessions 3-5. Reading the backstory on, The Academy, Blake Benton, and The Lunchroom will help students to understand the material and better answer the questions. In session 7, reading Will's bio will also be enlightening.
- Scripture verses for each session are printed at the end of the study guide. Due to the reflowable nature of ebooks, the page numbers of the ebook of this study are not the same *as those of the print version.* Please encourage those using the ebook to utilize the Table of Contents to navigate between book sections.
- *Chapter Summaries* and answers to the questions are included in the *Leader's Guide* section of this study.

15-MINUTE READING SELECTIONS FOR SESSIONS

Session 1: *Chapter Summaries* for Session 1and Chapter Two of *Run.*

Session 2: *Chapter Summaries* for Session 2 and Chapter Six of *Run.*

Session 3: *Chapter Summaries* for Sessions 3 & 4 and Chapter Eleven of *Run.*

Session 4: The first and last scenes of Chapter Twelve and the entire of Chapter Thirteen of *Run.* Also read the bio on Blake Benton in the *Cool Backstory & Fun*

Factoids. (Note: *Chapter Summaries* for this section were read in Session 3).

Session 5: *Chapter Summaries* for Session 5 and Chapter Seventeen of *Run*. Also read the description of the Lunchroom in the *Cool Backstory & Fun Factoids*.

Session 6: *Chapter Summaries* for Session 6 and Chapter Twenty-Four of *Run*.

Session 7: *Chapter Summaries* for Session 7 and Chapter Twenty-Seven of *Run*, (beginning with scene #2, the prayer meeting).

CHAPTER SUMMARIES

SESSION 1: *RUN* Chapters 1-5

Thirteen-year-old newbie, Tyler Higgins wants to prove himself to the older and cooler Matt Colter. So he searches for Matt's fort in the state parkland behind Tyler's new home. But while exploring the forested plateau, Tyler and his younger brother, Dylan, get lost. A wicked thunderstorm panics Dylan, and both boys fall into a ravine leaving Tyler with a minor concussion.

While looking for a way out, the brothers bump into an abandoned house and decide to go inside for shelter. They're not alone, and a creepy character begins searching the house for the boys. Somehow the brothers escape with Tyler re-injuring his head in the process. They find their way home, and Tyler swears Dylan to secrecy to avoid grounding from the forest.

The next morning, Tyler awakens with a throbbing headache and hardly believes the previous day's nightmare. Searching the forest is out of the question, so Tyler decides to prove himself to Matt by learning to fish the river. But today's Sunday, and Tyler must first navigate the next new social sphere—Church and Youth Group. Only the nerdy Luke wants to befriend Tyler and his brother, But Tyler does enlist Luke's help to fish the river.

A toothache forces Frank, one of the creeps from the ruined house, into Lehigh to find a dentist. While shopping for fishing gear in the local hardware store, Tyler and Dylan recognize the puffy jawed man's voice, sending shivers down their spines. The brothers escape detection and spy on the criminal, noting his suspicious purchases. Outside, Tyler discovers Frank drives a plumber's van.

After working up his courage, Tyler calls the phone number on the van. When a professional sounding woman answers, he hangs up mostly convinced Delta Plumbing is a legitimate business. But the plumbers Caller ID all their phone calls…

Tyler, Dylan and Luke finally get their fishing gear together and find a sweet spot beneath the river bridge. But from the bridge above, Matt and Ryan dump swamp muck on the fishermen. As the trio trudge home, Matt turned bully, holds them up and steals their fish.

SESSION 2: *RUN* Chapters 6-10

Tyler blames Luke for Matt's dirty trick, but Dylan comes to Luke's defense. Later Luke grosses Tyler out when he pretends to eat a bugger. When Tyler gets Dylan alone, he rants against Luke to his younger brother, but again Dylan sides with the husky boy. Thinking Luke had left, Tyler lets loose another, meaner tirade against the neighbor. Luke overhears the insults and stomps home, nearly provoking a fistfight between the brothers. Dylan is so mad at Tyler, the brothers are estranged.

Matt is a lost cause, and Dylan and Luke are shunning Tyler. So he retreats into the world of role player video games and fantasizes over a return to Florida. But after a week he's super bored. To avoid Dylan and Luke's rejection and Matt's persecution, he decides to sneak out of the house at night.

That first night, Tyler finds a comfortable spot by the river bridge and tries to talk to God. But he's not ready to forgive Luke. As a dark van approaches the bridge, Tyler hides and recognizes the Delta Plumbing van. Over the next several nights he spies on the van, and on the fifth night, feelings of menace propel Tyler home. On the way, a huge man with a long knife threatens Tyler and his family if he doesn't stop spying.

Still dazed and scared witless the next morning, Tyler decides he can't tell anyone about the plumber for fear the brute will kill his mother and sister. Mom reminds Tyler that school starts on the morrow. At school the next day it doesn't go well. Dylan ditches Tyler, and seeking a spot to hole up, Tyler trips and almost falls in front of a crowd of girls. Knowing no one, Tyler must wait for school to start—alone.

When the building finally opens, Tyler can't unlock his locker and must obtain help from the office. Arriving to class late, he finds a room full of complete strangers, all gawking at him. Although one boy seems friendly, the kids turn hostile when they discover Tyler's an outsider and accuse his father of stealing local jobs. Tyler survives the day, but happens upon Blake, the school bully picking on a little kid. Tyler escapes the resulting confrontation but fears the bully has marked him for trouble.

SESSIONS 3 & 4: *RUN* Chapters 11-15

Ninth-grader, Blake Benton, and two of Tyler's eighth-grade classmates, Nick and Carlos, single Tyler out for bullying. Tyler ignores Blake's initial challenge and taunts and retreats to the adult supervised student pickup area where the bully is reluctant to start anything. And the next day, Tyler asks Mom to time his morning drop off so he can go straight to class and avoid having to hang around outside where adult supervision is sparse. Still, Nick taunts Tyler when the teacher leaves the room. Tyler returns the insults and backs Nick down. But Nick vows revenge and the older Blake promises to give Tyler a pounding. Later that day, Blake "accidentally" bumps into Tyler in the hall, but Tyler was ready for it and bumps back, knocking the bully off balance, Tyler keeps moving and avoids further confrontation. Then by staying alert in the following days, Tyler avoids Blake's ambushes and schemes to catch him without adult supervision.

On Saturday, Tyler holes up in his bedroom playing video games. But the weather is nice, and Dad kicks him outside. While wandering a near trail in the opposite direction from the ruined house, Tyler meets a new boy. Will is Tyler's age, attends another school and is visiting his father, Doc Fuller, who lives on a near ridge overlooking the valley. But Tyler can't figure out why Will was crying. After returning home, Dylan enjoys reminding Tyler that Blake the bully is still hunting him.

Tyler decides to prepare for the worst with Blake and breaks out the heavy bag to work on his boxing technique. Dad reminds Tyler of his no fighting policy and after a heart to heart, Tyler learns what he knew all along, Dad is an ally. Tyler also discovers that Will's mom is in a coma from a car accident. That's why Will is so sad and is temporarily staying with his father. Tyler decides to start talking to God again, to pray for his enemies and for Will. He also decides to revisit Will.

A tropical storm blows far inland and unaware of the flooding, Mom charges Tyler with walking Dylan and Rachael to school. Dylan drops his music pod as he crosses the river bridge, and while trying to retrieve the device, he falls. At the last instant, a garage door, ripped off by the flood materializes, providing a raft for Dylan. But the debris could capsize any second. After a desperate prayer, Tyler runs ahead, shinnies out on a tree limb and plucks Dylan off the onrushing raft.

Dylan and Tyler are reconciled. Tyler has his bro back and begins attending youth group. However, a couple of girls from The Academy show up and disrespect Tyler. Under conviction, Tyler wants to request prayer for Will, but fear of the girls' gossip at school keeps him silent.

SESSION 5: ***RUN*** Chapters 16-20

Meanwhile, the flood provides a bonanza for the plumbers. After the plumbers loot deserted houses miles downstream from Lehigh, a cop becomes suspicious. Using their telephone technology, the two burglars fool the cop temporarily. But soon they discover that the officer is investigating Delta Plumbing. Although the corporation conceals the true owners and their location, Runyon determines they only have another week before they must shut down operations. They decide to tackle the big heist they've been planning for months.

When school reopens on Thursday with light attendance, Blake and his posse finally corner Tyler in the lunchroom—alone. Tyler tries to talk his way out but is forced to defend himself and defeats Blake with surprising ease. All seems well until the headmaster hears Blake's lies and confronts Tyler. With no other witnesses and Blake's two friends covering for him, the headmaster blames Tyler. Immediate detention, possible suspension and even expulsion are Tyler's punishment.

Tyler braves the final day of the week at The Academy and finds his classmate's animosity ratcheted up a notch. The headmaster adds humiliating consequences to Tyler's after-school detention. Tyler perseveres and visits Will on Saturday, finding a kindred gaming spirit. Tyler even shares his faith a little—but then backs down. At the end of the visit, Will grows distant, and Tyler wonders if he's failed again.

After church the next day at Subway, Tyler runs into Matt, whom he hasn't seen in a month. Expecting another bullying, Tyler is surprised when Matt sides with him against Blake. A friend of Matt's has recently gone missing, and Matt confesses new information about the ditching in the woods. He warns Tyler away from the forest. Tyler imagines the plumber is responsible but says nothing to Matt. At home, Tyler still sweats over his visit with Will until Will invites Tyler to his house for breakfast the next day.

Late Sunday night, Frank and Runyon hit Fat Cat's house. Using computers, high-tech jamming gear, and a legendary knockout gas from the Russian mob, the two burglars bag millions in cash and jewelry. Although surveillance cameras will compromise their Delta Plumbing cover, the criminals figure they have time for one more job. This one is personal.

SESSION 6: *RUN* Chapters 21-24

After a night of nightmares featuring the plumber, Tyler arises and treks up the mountain to meet Will for Breakfast. Near the crest of the ridge, he sees the Delta Plumbing van motoring up Will's driveway from the opposite side. Runyon and Frank plan on emptying Doc Fuller's house that very morning.

However, the doctor returns and the plumbers pretend they are lost and take their leave, vowing to return that night. Tyler is relieved to find Will and his dad are okay. But he's scared witless and after a lame excuse runs for home without warning the Fullers of his fears.

Tyler hides out in his room for the rest of that Monday. After school the next day he discovers the Fullers had been burglarized the night before. Hit on the head, Doctor Fuller lays in the hospital in a coma along with his wife. Will, who slept through the robbery, is okay. Crushed with guilt, Tyler confesses his knowledge to Will, Luke and Dylan. When Tyler tells the tale of the ruined house, Will decides to find the hideout, call the police on his cell phone and recover his mother's jewelry. Tyler agrees to lead him there.

Tyler, Dylan, Luke and Will retrace the trail through the woods to the plumber's hideout. Will knows the maze of dirt roads on the plateau and can identify the location. But first they must get closer and pass the driveway to see the road beyond. After sneaking past the garage with a creepy digging sound on the other side, Will identifies the road. On the way back out, the boys witness the two plumbers, Frank and Runyon, burying a body. Then as they watch, the men fall into mortal combat with Runyon and his long knife prevailing. Luke screams, Runyon sees the boys, and they run.

Climbing a steep ridge, the boys at first seem to be escaping. But the big man isn't as fat as he first appeared. He closes in, and Tyler realizes that Luke and Will cannot escape. Refusing to leave them behind, Tyler sends the boys ahead and decoys the plumber on a side trail. But the plumber is faster than Tyler, and soon he closes in. After shooting up a prayer, Tyler takes to a large, climbable tree. While the one armed man tries in vain to climb the tree, goaded on by Tyler, the three other boys escape. Realizing he's been fooled, the plumber in a rage flings his knife at Tyler.

SESSION 7: *RUN* Chapters 25-27

Tyler dodges the knife. With one last bellow of rage, Runyon descends the slope back to his hideout. Tyler runs for home to find everyone safe. Meanwhile, the plumber stuffs his duffle bags with money and escapes to the river. Vowing revenge, he heads toward a small island not far from Tyler's house. He plans to visit Tyler and his family in the dead of night. Meanwhile, the police interview Tyler and decide to leave a squad car to guard his house.

Hiding half buried on the sandy island, Runyon eludes pursuit until midnight. He stabs the officer guarding Tyler's house and advances toward the back door with his silencer screwed tight on his 9mm. But awakened by another bad dream, Tyler catches sight of the big man as he passes beneath the street light. Racing to the back door, Tyler has another plan to lead the killer away from those he loves. Outside, Tyler dials 9-1-1 on the mobile phone, hails Runyon and runs into the night dodging bullets. The big man pursues, but just as he's about to lay hands on Tyler, police sirens rend the air. Fleeing back toward the house—and his money, Runyon is finally cornered and captured by police.

After another interview with the deputy, Tyler learns that the patrolman Runyon attacked still lives, but Doc Fuller remains in a coma. At Luke's house later that day, Tyler invites Will to join them at youth group that night for special prayer. Will agrees. The youth group joins the adults in the church's main auditorium where a large crowd—much of the town—have gathered to pray for the Fullers and the stricken deputy Fox. Under conviction, Tyler confesses some things, forgives

Audrey and prays with thanksgiving. The prayer meeting ended with anticipation. In the climax, Tyler is called to the hospital the next day to find that both Will's dad *and mom* are awake and well. And Tyler finally has a new friend, one now interested in the Lord.

ANSWER GUIDE

SESSION 1: Finding Friends

Ice Breakers – personal experience opinion answers

Search the Scriptures

1. People generally don't like hanging out with people who think they are superior.

2. All believers are God's children and one in Christ. All are of equal value to God.

3. No Scripture Reference. When others get too clingy, people feel smothered and generally respond by avoiding that person.

4. Through a relationship with Jesus, we can be content when alone because we are never alone in Christ. And Jesus provides the power to wait until God provides other companionship.

5. Be content by:
   a) Giving thanks to God for the positive things you have
   b) Asking God for what you need (companionship)
   c) Thinking and talking about good things (v 8)

d) Continuing to study God's word like we are doing right now

6. This question is a challenge to action.

Read the *How Will You Respond* section aloud to the students.

SESSION 2: Forgiving Friends

Ice Breakers – personal experience opinion answers

Search the Scriptures

1. We need to focus on listening. And when getting angry, it's best to hold our tongues and wait until we can control our emotions. Sometimes that means walking away.

2. We as believers must forgive others because the Lord forgives us and commands us to do the same. And, forgiveness usually leads to reconciliation – restored friendships.

3. People often say mean things when angry, which further strains relationships and is always what the devil wants. If not resolved, anger also leads to bitterness.

4. Bitterness makes people sad and leads to complaining, more anger and even revenge. Bitter people are usually unpleasant to be around.

5. Personal question, but saying something nice to the person who has offended you goes far to heal relationships. And healed relationships make us happy!

Also, when we pray for someone, not only does it release the power of God in his or her life, it's also usually then hard for us to remain angry with that person.

6. Tyler thought Luke had turned Matt against him, and now he thought Luke would steal Dylan's friendship away as well. But it turned out that neither of these thoughts was true.

7. God doesn't forgive us. By refusing to forgive Luke, and *showing* forgiveness by accepting him in friendship, Tyler alienated both Luke and his brother Dylan. And Tyler ended up alone.

Read the *How Will You Respond*, section aloud to the students. Maybe add, "What does forgiveness look like in how you treat the offending person?"

SESSION 3: Facing Bullies — Part 1

Search the Scriptures

Read each tip aloud.

1. a) The God of the universe created every person in His image, regardless of his or her ethnicity or characteristics. We are all precious to God. Therefore, hurting others, or allowing others to hurt us, dishonors God. This includes verbal abuse, see also James 3:8-10.

1. b) The bullying that bullies dish out will return to them in some form of judgment, often they are bullied in turn.

1. c) God wants everyone, including bullies to repent—change their mind and ways. He often withholds justice to give people an opportunity to do so.

1. d) Ask for God's help. Psalm 139:23–24 says, *"Search me, O God, and know my heart; test me and know my anxious thoughts. Point out anything in me that offends you, and lead me along the path of everlasting life."* Counter lying thoughts and words with a "no," and reciting the truth in our minds. Renounce and replace. Recalling memorized Scripture has a powerful positive effect when confronted with self lies. Try to hang out with people who are positive and avoid those who are negative or like to run people down. Think about good things, like a hobby or something else fun and positive.

2. a) This is a personal question, but prayer often helps us to forgive and removes anger. Blessing encourages those who hear the blessing and often convicts the person doing the bullying to be nice.

3. a) When confronted with danger, he relocated to an area where there were adults (better explained in *Run* chapter 11). So avoid (if you can) places where bullies are likely to roam, especially places without adult supervision. Tyler also had his mom time his drop off at school so he wouldn't have to hang around outside with minimal or no adult supervision.

4. a) Tyler said nothing when first confronted by Blake, he avoided him by retreating to the after-school pickup area. Not so much when Nick insulted him later in the chapter (see question c)

4. b) Harsh words make people angrier. On the other hand, a gentle answer often can defuse the situation, and turn another's meanness away.

4. c) Tyler called Nick "pepperoni face" and a "coward." But Nick only became angrier and vowed revenge. Speculate: Nick probably would have kept up the verbal taunting. Unlikely, but he might have let it go and left Tyler alone. Or he might have escalated to physical abuse anyway and might have been caught at it by the teacher. The study answers the question of *how* Tyler could have responded to Nick but without retaliation in the next tip (read the next tip).

5. a) Generally responding with a question, rather than name calling, or a confrontational statement that leaves the bully's most likely response as one of further hostility.

6. a) Generally places where adults are present, the library, cafeteria normally, study hall rooms. Avoid the bathroom between classes and rather ask for a pass during class. Outside, you might lock yourself inside your parent's car for example.

6. b) Bullies typically look for weakness; when your back is turned, you are an easy target.

7. a) This is a personal answer, but again answers should be sincere and specific compliments, like "nice (whatever), I like (this or that) about it." for an art or craft project. Or "great game (give details athletically)." Or, compliment their clothing, or other material possession, their taste, etc. Be observant, and you can always find something nice to say.

Read the *How Will You Respond,* section aloud to the students. Ask the questions therein and be ready to investigate and intervene if you determine that bullying is actually taking place.

SESSION 4: Facing Bullies — Part 2

Ice Breaker – personal experience answers

Search the Scriptures

Read each tip aloud.

8. a) Speculate. School officials probably would have investigated the charge and brought Blake to account, which would have improved Tyler's situation. On the other hand, it might have just made Blake madder and more determined to catch Tyler off campus.

8. b) Encourage students to share any bullying they are experiencing with the group, or leader afterward. Also encourage them to commit to telling their parents, or school or other officials.

9. a) Tyler stood up to Nick in class, but because he retaliated, it increased the hostility. He stood up to Blake in the hallway, by using a subtle self-defense technique against what would have been a mild physical attack (a shoulder bump to knock Tyler back or down). The maneuver might have gained Tyler some respect, but it only made Blake more determined to bully Tyler. Sometimes doing what was arguably the right thing can still lead to negative consequences. You can ask the group the question, "what might have happened if Tyler let Blake knock him over?"

9. b) Listen to and encourage the personal responses and sharing of the results. Otherwise, make the question hypothetical. This strategy generally works when there is a larger crowd including people not in the bully's click, especially older students or adults who might intervene. It could be less effective in a smaller group that consists of the bully's posse, and/or the student's peers only.

9. c) Yes, because it's the right thing to do, and because if a bully is targeting someone else, and gets away with it, what's to stop him or her from targeting you next time? There is no single right answer as to which tip (strategy) to employ first. If you have the nerve, speak up loudly, "Are you bullying that person?" If they say "no" they will probably back off. If they say "yes" follow up with another question, "what will blank authorities think about that?" and/or "how do you know someone isn't videoing you right now?" Or if you can't get up the nerve on the spot, tell a responsible adult. These things are often unexpected, when they happen, role play how you will respond the next time. And don't forget to be kind to the person who is bullied.

10. a) When a weapon is involved such as a knife, club of some sort, or gun. When a gang known for violence is involved, and when older kids or adults are involved in the bullying. What are some others?

10. b) Blake didn't pursue Tyler fearing adult intervention or getting caught in the open area with lots of witnesses. If Blake had a weapon, dial 911—call the police.

10. c) Draw out answers, then read the *How Will You Respond* section following for advice on cyberbullying.

The matter often should be reported to the forum authorities, school officials or police.

Read all of the *How Will You Respond* section and point out the resources on the next page.

SESSION 5: Facing Bullies — Part 3

Search the Scriptures

1. No, he rebuked the person who struck him.
2. Yes, believers should defend the persecuted weak, but how to defend depends upon the context and the power the believer has at his or her disposal.
3. Yes, physical force, but non-lethal.
4. Yes, and Jesus commanded them to arm themselves.
5. Peace isn't always possible because if an aggressor does not agree to peace, then one person or party can perform the violence regardless of what the other party does.
6. No, revenge is prohibited. However, governmental retribution is another matter. According to Romans 13:1-6, God gave governments the right to have laws and deal out punishment for wrong, but often more as a deterrent to future crime, and to protect society.

7. "Don't extort money or make false accusations. And be content with your pay." No.

8. If you resort to violence for any reason, you should expect to incur violent harm—eventually.

Read *How Will You Respond*, including the questions contained therein.

> Yes. Tyler prepared himself for self-defense (see *Chapter Summaries* for Sessions 3 &4).

SESSION 6: Sacrifice for Friends

Search the Scriptures

1. Tyler shot up a "Lord, help," prayer while on the run with the murderer closing in on him. God provided a tree and the idea to climb it. Tyler hadn't yet even considered how the big man's one arm would prevent him from following.

2. Defer to others. For example, if you love soccer and your friend doesn't, or even has a handicap, you could decide not to play soccer and do something that your friend would like.

3. Read the list to yourself and pick your own answers and share with the group if the discussion bogs down.

4. Same as question 3.

5. Same as question 3.

6. Think about the other person first. Think of how he or she would feel if you said something negative about them. Another countermeasure is to imagine the person

you are tempted to disrespect is in the room and listening.

7. We can forgive because we have been forgiven. Often we've done the very things we'd hate to have done to us.

8. Encourage others, say nice things to them and about them. Again, sincere compliments are always fun and healing. Ask their opinion on something and look them in the eye and listen when they talk. This demonstrates that you think they have worth, that their opinions have value—even if you don't agree!

Read the *How Will You Respond* section and the question at the end ("List one action step . . .").

SESSION 7: Talk to God

Search the Scriptures

1. As our father. God sees us as his beloved children!

2. When God's Kingdom comes, evil will be removed; believers will be made perfect and perfectly connected to God in his presence. As perfect beings, people will obey God and be connected to one another with love and joy and no conflict. Aligning with God's will means surrendering our will and desires to God and attempting to do his will. Ask for examples.

3. God's children. Students can be sure they are God's children if they receive Jesus in faith according to John 1:12. In addition, you can also explain the gospel and give the students an opportunity to trust in Jesus. Or

you can ask your pastor for help. You can also read 1 John 5:13 and other verses on assurance.

4. a. 1 John 1:9 = Confession

   b. Matthew 7:7-8 = Making requests

   c. Ephesians 5:20 = Thanksgiving

   d. Psalm 103:1-2 = Praise

5. Harboring willful and unconfessed sin in our heart hinders our prayers to God. If we want God to hear us, we should confess known sins (but only once). Once confessed, God ALWAYS immediately forgives our sins (1 John 1:9).

6. Personal answers. Leaders can always share their own answers if the discussion lags.

7. a. James 5:13. Pray when in any kind of trouble.

   b. Philippians 4:6. Pray when we are worried.

   c. Matthew 26:41. Pray when tempted.

8. If we ask for anything that is in accord with God's will, God will do it, for he always does what he wills. Therefore, we should first try to determine God's will. The Bible and God's promises are keys to determining his will. We are commanded to pray for our needs (Matthew 6:11), but we shouldn't expect God to give us jealous and selfish prayer requests, especially requests that will ultimately harm us physically or morally.

9. Tyler confessed his own sins and forgave Audrey. He asked God to heal Will's parents and the injured sheriff's deputy, both unselfish and good requests. The story also records Tyler's thankfulness for his new

friends and God's forgiveness. Although praise isn't mentioned specifically, the prayer meeting included worship.

Read the *How Will You Respond* section and the question at the end (the opening questions are rhetorical, so you don't need to get an answer). How much time do you spend in alert prayer per day? If the students are reluctant to answer, the leader can again answer it from his or her own life.

Note: In addition to CRU's gospel explanation (see the link in Session 7), Focus on the Family has an excellent explanation of how to join God's family. Although designed for adults, it provides helpful insight into a believer's relationship to God. Session 7 might be a good place to raise that issue. Check it out at: **www.focusonthefamily.com/faith/becoming-a-christian/coming-home-an-invitation-to-join-gods-family**

Did you enjoy this study?

If so, would you take a quick minute to leave a review? It needn't be long. Just a sentence or two saying what you liked about the study!

Your recommendation would be a huge encouragement to me and help others to find this book.

www.amazon.com/dp/B07F1JNBMT

Be the first to know about new books by Glenn Haggerty!

Get the inside scoop and occasional freebies through Glenn's newsletter, INTENSE.

Signup for INTENSE Email Updates

www.glennh[illegible]/get-intense/

Check out the books in Glenn Haggerty's

Intense Series

Escape

Intense Book 1

Run

Intense Book 2

Chase

Intense Book 3

About the Author

Glenn has a Master of Divinity degree from Bethel Seminary. He is an award-winning author who combines his love for teaching God's word with his passion for writing exciting fiction.

In addition to the action adventure novel, *Run* (Intense Book 2), he has published two additional books in his Intense series, *Escape* (Book 1) and *Chase* (Book 3). Eight of his short stories have appeared in six magazines, including Cadet Quest, Partners, Splickety, and Havok.

Glenn is a member of American Christian Fiction Writers, a graduate of Vision Loss Resources and Bethel Seminary, father of six, and grandfather of seven. He lives in Minneapolis with his wife and enjoys tandem biking and kayaking.

You can visit Glenn on his website at
www.glennhaggerty.com.

www.ingramcontent.com/pod-product-compliance
Lightning Source LLC
Chambersburg PA
CBHW020513030426
42337CB00011B/363

* 9 7 8 0 9 9 9 3 9 9 4 5 3 *